The River Book

Dr Brian Knapp

Atlantic Europe Publishing

First published in 1998 by
Atlantic Europe Publishing Company Ltd

Author
Brian Knapp, BSc, PhD
Art Director
Duncan McCrae, BSc
Editors
Elizabeth Walker, BA, and Mary Sanders, BSc
Illustrations
David Woodroffe
Designed and produced by
EARTHSCAPE EDITIONS
Reproduced in Malaysia by
Global Colour
Printed and bound in Italy by
L.E.G.O. SpA

Suggested cataloguing location
Knapp, Brian
 The River Book
 1. Rivers – Juvenile Literature
 I. Title. (Series: *Curriculum visions*)
551.483

ISBN 1 862140 00 6 Hardback
ISBN 1 862140 05 7 Paperback

Picture credits
All photographs are from the Earthscape
Editions photolibrary except the following:
(c=centre t=top b=bottom l=left r=right)
Prof Denys Brunsden 31tl; FEMA 39tr, 39b,
43t, 43br; NASA 27tr, 27cr.

*This product is manufactured from sustainable
managed forests. For every tree cut down at least
one more is planted.*

Niagara Falls, Canada

Curriculum Visions

Glossary
There is a glossary on page 47. Glossary terms are referred to in the text by using CAPITALS like this.

Index
There is an index on page 48.

There's more on the Web
This is a web-linked book. You will find more free information, photographs and detail about topics in this book by visiting our world wide web site:

www.CurriculumVisions.com

Take care near rivers!
It is easy to visit streams and rivers to see for yourself many of the landshapes described in this book. But remember streams and rivers can be dangerous places so <u>never</u> take risks near deep water, or go near a river when it is raining heavily and floods are likely.

There is a **teacher's guide**, **river adventure stories** and other support material to accompany this book. These are available from the publisher.

River Contents

Upper Yosemite Falls, USA

Features of rivers and valleys

These are the *natural* features you might expect to see in a river valley.

1 The **SOURCE** is the origin of a river. It may be a **SPRING** in a hillside hollow or melting snow in a mountain. The source is also known as the **HEADWATERS**. A more detailed description is on page 8.

2 The **RIVER BASIN** (also called the drainage basin) is the whole area that is drained by a river. River basins are also on page 8.

3 Branches, or **TRIBUTARIES** are the smaller rivers and streams that feed into the main river. These are also shown on page 8.

4 A **WATERFALL** occurs where a river falls over a **CLIFF**. Find out how waterfalls work on page 16.

5 In some places a river will contain many small shifting islands, find out about **BRAIDED RIVERS** on page 22.

6 A **MEANDER** is a large curve or loop in a river. Meanders are shown on page 18.

7 Where meanders have been cut through, old channels may remain filled with water and form **OXBOW LAKES**. These are on page 20.

8 In some places a **LAKE** may form where, for example, water is ponded back behind natural obstacles such as rock bars, or because land was scoured out by ancient glaciers. Find out about lakes on page 24.

9 A **GORGE** is a part of the valley where the river runs between cliff-like sides. See this on page 28.

10 A **DELTA** is an area of land made by a river as it enters the sea or a lake. Deltas are shown on page 26.

11 An **ESTUARY** is a place where a river enters the sea in a 'drowned' valley. More information on estuaries is on pages 26 and 36.

12 The **UPPER VALLEY** usually has steeply sloping sides and **INTERLOCKING SPURS**. A description is on page 32.

13 The **MIDDLE VALLEY** has a **FLOODPLAIN** formed in a valley that has moderately steep sides. Sometimes it has benches called **RIVER TERRACES**. See this on page 34.

14 The **LOWER VALLEY** has a wide floodplain and the sides have very gentle slopes. The floodplain sometimes has **LEVEES** (natural riverside embankments). This is shown on page 36.

Source **1**

Lake **8**

The river basin **2**
is the whole
area drained
by the river

Steep slopes and
interlocking spurs **12**
in the upper
regions of a valley

Waterfall
4

Gorge below
9 waterfall

Braided
river **5**

Tributary
3

13
Moderately steep slopes
in the middle regions of a
valley. Levees possible on
floodplain beside the river.

Meandering river
6

7
Oxbow lake

Gentle slopes in **14**
the lower regions
of a valley

10 and **11**
Deltas and
estuaries

How people use rivers and valleys

These are some of the *man-made* features you might expect to see where people make use of a river and its valley.

1 Many cities were built next to rivers to carry goods or for defence. Many cities also grew up at places where the river was easy to cross, either by bridge or ferry. Unfortunately these riverside settlements are at risk from flooding. See this on page 38.

As cities grew, so more soil was covered with houses and roads. This added to the risk of flooding. Find out why on page 40.

Within cities, river banks are built up. This makes the river narrower and increases the chances of floods, as you will see on page 41.

2 Valley-side settlements were built to keep away from the floodplain. But valley-side slopes are difficult to build on, so few of these places have grown into cities.

3 The floodplain is used for farmland because of its fertility. However, the crops may be destroyed when the land floods. See widespread flooding on page 38.

4 Valley sides are often used for pasture. They were once forested. Taking away forests makes flooding more likely. The way this happens is shown on page 40.

5 Dams, reservoirs and levees can be used to keep floods from farmland and cities. Why they are used is described on page 42.

6 Bridges are used to cross rivers, but they can partly block the flow of water and help to cause floods.

7 Water is often diverted from rivers and taken by canal (**AQUEDUCT**) to irrigate (water) fields and as drinking water for cities. This is shown on page 44.

8 **WATER PURIFICATION** is necessary before river water can be drunk. Waste water (sewage) must be cleaned before it is returned to the river. See the diagram on page 44.

9 If untreated waste is released into a river, it can pollute the water for long distances.

10 Lakes and reservoirs are used for recreation, but their main use is to store water, to prevent floods and to generate electricity. See this on page 44.

11 Many cities were built near to the coast to make use of a sheltered harbour in the river mouth. To do this they have often had to **RECLAIM LAND** from a delta or estuary.

12 Farmers need to use large amounts of water for irrigation during dry weather. You can see this on page 45.

13 Gravel is often extracted from the floodplain and used as a building material.

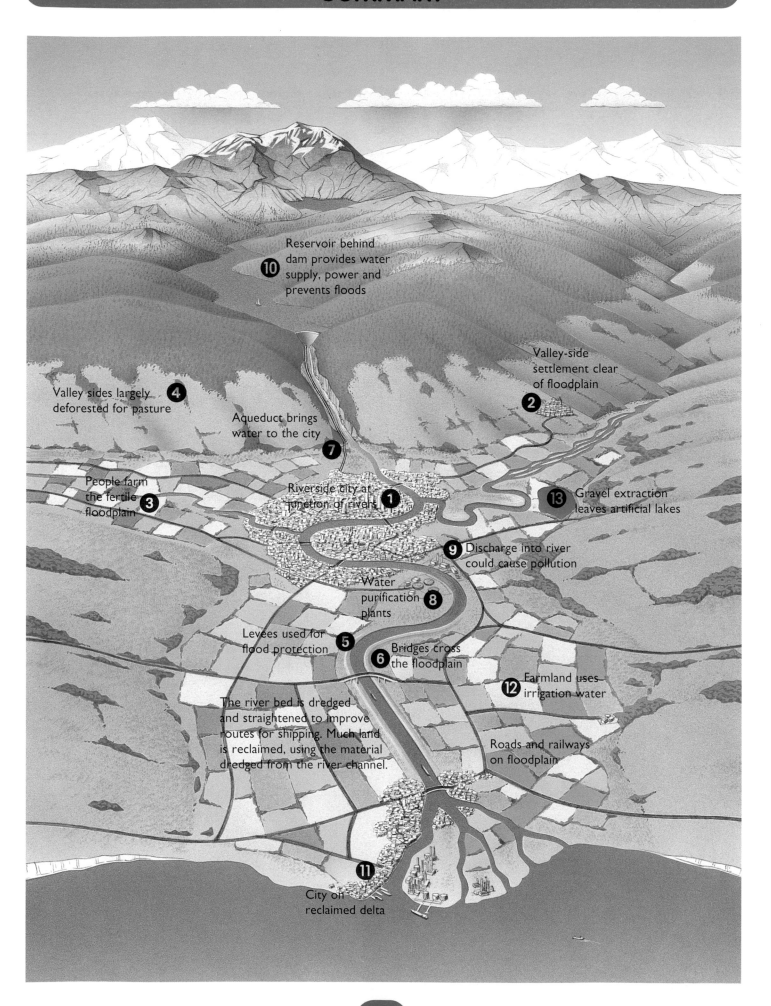

Reservoir behind dam provides water supply, power and prevents floods — ⑩

Valley-side settlement clear of floodplain — ②

Valley sides largely deforested for pasture — ④

Aqueduct brings water to the city — ⑦

People farm the fertile floodplain — ③

Riverside city at junction of rivers — ①

Gravel extraction leaves artificial lakes — ⑬

Discharge into river could cause pollution — ⑨

Water purification plants — ⑧

Levees used for flood protection — ⑤

Bridges cross the floodplain — ⑥

Farmland uses irrigation water — ⑫

The river bed is dredged and straightened to improve routes for shipping. Much land is reclaimed, using the material dredged from the river channel.

Roads and railways on floodplain

City on reclaimed delta — ⑪

Where rivers get their water

The water cycle provides rivers with water whether it rains or not.

Rivers flow even in times of **DROUGHT**. So where do rivers get their water?

The answer lies in the **WATER CYCLE**, the constant sharing of water between the land, the oceans and the air (picture ①).

▼ ① The water cycle carries water from oceans to air to clouds to rain to soil and rocks, then rivers and back to the sea. Notice that a drainage basin, river and tributaries are also shown here.

Making clouds and rain

If you leave a saucer of water out on a windowledge, the water will soon disappear. In just the same way, dry air soaks up water from the oceans as vapour. This is called **EVAPORATION**.

Vapour makes the air moist. Near the ground, the air is relatively warm and can hold a lot of vapour. As the moist air rises, it reaches much colder regions high in the sky. These regions

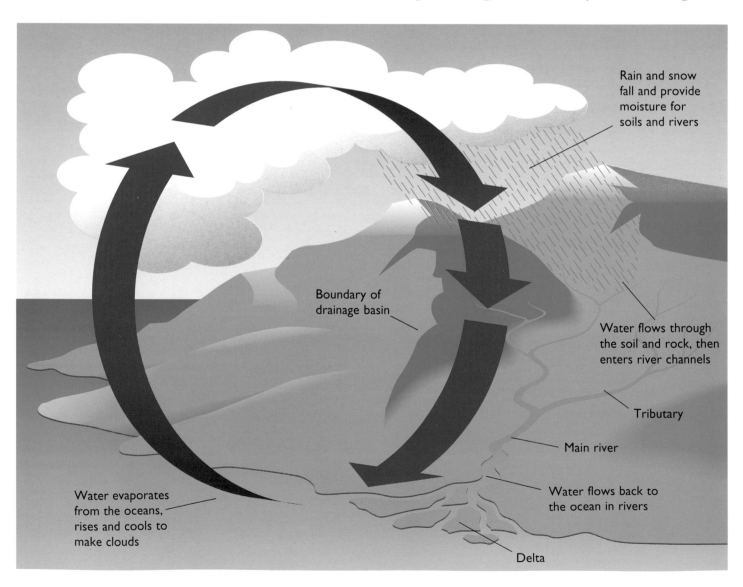

Rain and snow fall and provide moisture for soils and rivers

Boundary of drainage basin

Water flows through the soil and rock, then enters river channels

Tributary

Main river

Water evaporates from the oceans, rises and cools to make clouds

Water flows back to the ocean in rivers

Delta

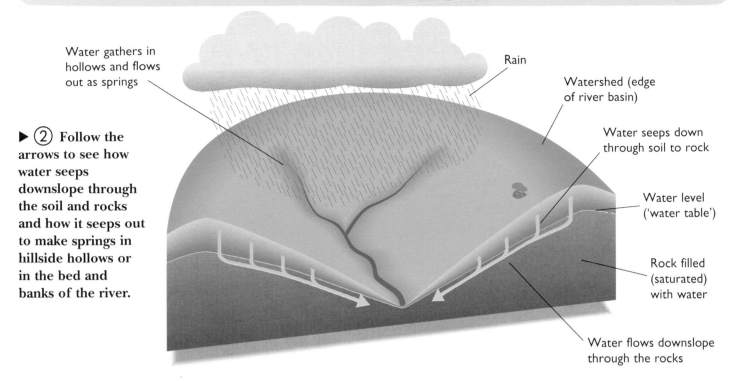

Water gathers in hollows and flows out as springs

Rain

Watershed (edge of river basin)

Water seeps down through soil to rock

Water level ('water table')

Rock filled (saturated) with water

Water flows downslope through the rocks

▶ ② **Follow the arrows to see how water seeps downslope through the soil and rocks and how it seeps out to make springs in hillside hollows or in the bed and banks of the river.**

can hold much less moisture, so as the air rises, the vapour changes into droplets or even ice crystals. We see the droplets and crystals as clouds.

Inside clouds, droplets and ice crystals group together until they are heavy enough to fall to the ground. Then it rains or snows.

From rain to river

Most rainfall seeps into the soil and moves underground – it very rarely runs across the soil surface. Soil and rock acts as a giant sponge. Water seeps slowly down through this natural sponge, where much of it is stored (picture ②).

When many of the spaces (pores) in the soils and rocks are filled with water, the water seeps out. Sometimes it forms a spring (picture ③), but some water simply seeps out through the river bank or bed. This water

feeds the river between rainstorms. Water in the soil is also used by plants.

Finally, river water flows back to the ocean to complete the water cycle.

Of course, if there are several months without rain, the plants use up the water from the soils and all the surplus water drains out of the rocks, so rivers will eventually dry up.

▲ ③ **This hot spring gushes out of the rock through a deep crack. Big springs are not common, however.**

How rivers wear away rocky beds

Two stages are needed to wear away a rock bed: the solid rock must first be worn down into smaller pieces, then it must be carried away.

Water cannot wear away, or **ERODE**, the land quickly on its own. It needs some form of scraping tool to work with. This is why pebbles and gravel are important. But they are so heavy, they can only be carried by the fastest of streams and rivers, like those shown in pictures ① and ③.

Fast-flowing water

You expect to see fast-flowing water in mountains and other places where the river rushes through a steep valley. Picture ② shows what happens.

You can imagine the water as a kind of liquid sandpaper. The fast-flowing water gives the energy, and the pebbles and gravel (picture ④) are the material used by the water to scrape at the bed.

▲ ① This is a typical mountain river. Water is swirling among the rocky ledges and boulders.

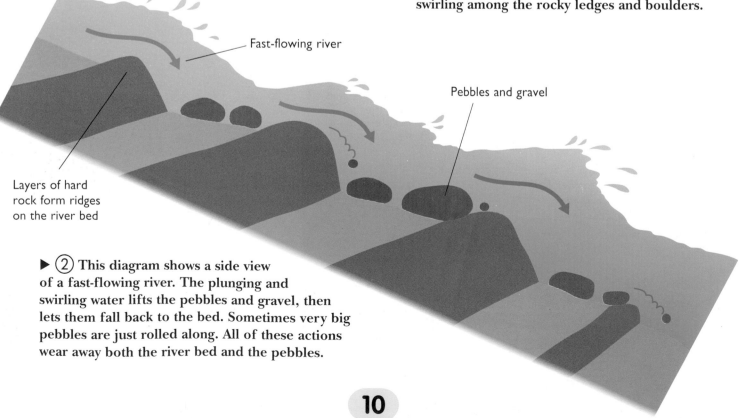

Fast-flowing river

Pebbles and gravel

Layers of hard rock form ridges on the river bed

▶ ② This diagram shows a side view of a fast-flowing river. The plunging and swirling water lifts the pebbles and gravel, then lets them fall back to the bed. Sometimes very big pebbles are just rolled along. All of these actions wear away both the river bed and the pebbles.

10

◀ ③ When the river level is low, such as in summer, the rocky bed shows clearly. The air bubbles trapped in the swirling and tumbling water gives it a white colour, and so it is described as 'white water'.

▶ ④ These are the materials you might find on the bed of a white water river. The pebbles are rounded from scraping across the bed. The technical word for scraping is ABRASION.

As the pebbles and river bed wear each other away, small pieces of rock break free. This produces the sand you can see in the picture.

All these pebbles will, in time, become tiny pieces of sand, SILT or mud. The word ATTRITION is used for the way pebbles wear each other down by bumping together in fast-moving water.

Potholes

A curious feature of some white water river beds are the natural holes – called potholes – hollowed out by spinning pebbles.

Canoeists who ride fast-flowing rivers of white water know how much they get tossed about, especially in the pools where water swirls.

When water swirls around and around it is called an **EDDY** (picture ①). If a pebble gets caught in an eddy it has difficulty in escaping. But as the pebble is heavy, it will spin around at the bottom of the river, and as it does so it will scrape against the bed, wearing away at the rock. If eddies become fixed in one place for a long time, then **POTHOLES** are drilled in the bed (picture ②).

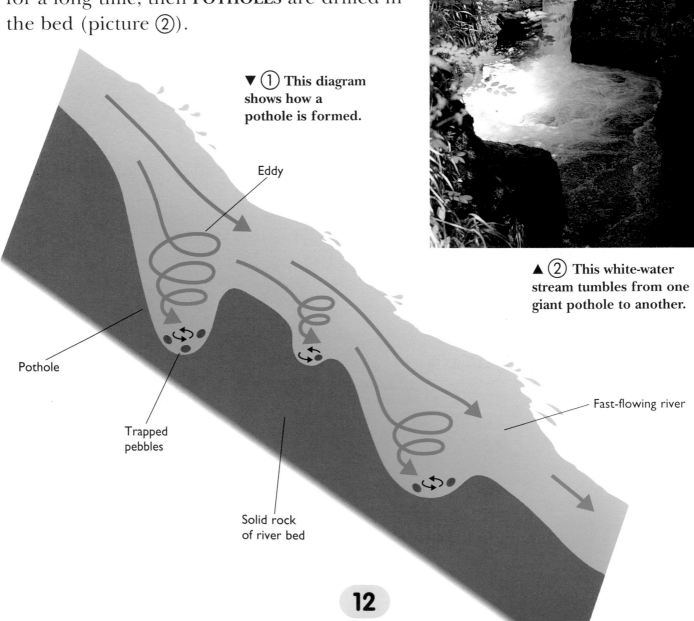

▼ ① This diagram shows how a pothole is formed.

Eddy

Pothole

Trapped pebbles

Solid rock of river bed

Fast-flowing river

▲ ② This white-water stream tumbles from one giant pothole to another.

What a pothole is like

A pothole is literally a pot-shaped hole, round and with near upright sides (pictures ③ and ④). It has been drilled out of the river bed by pebbles trapped in an eddy, scraping and chipping at the rock (picture ⑤).

Pebbles only escape when they have worn themselves down to tiny pieces. You will only find potholes in white water rivers with rocky beds.

▲ ③ These are potholes worn into the bed by pebbles trapped in the swirling water. It may take centuries for these deep holes to be formed: even in white-water conditions, changes are not that fast!

Erosion

The geographer's word for wearing away <u>and</u> removing natural material is **EROSION**. So, for example, a river erodes its bed and banks. The erosion taking place here happens through the wearing away of the bed by pebbles and the swift removal of fine pebble chips (sand) by the white water.

▼ ④ Here, at a time of low water, you can see the pebbles that wear the pothole away. These pebbles are not moving: potholes only form when the river is full and flowing swiftly, and then they are difficult to see.

▶ ⑤ This pebble was found in the bottom of a pothole. It has been worn down to a shape almost like a ball.

How rivers carry material away

Rivers drag, bounce, suspend and dissolve the materials they move.

The pebbles, sand and mud that you see on many river beds have been carried by the river before settling out on the bed. So they tell of material on the move (picture ①). However, if you look into a river, it will most likely be clear and nothing will seem to be moving at all. How, then, do the materials move?

Rivers move most of their material when the water is flowing unusually quickly, for example, during a flood.

In floods, the swirling river pushes pebbles along. This disturbs the river bed, allowing the water to sweep up sand and mud hidden below the pebbles, and carry it away. At the end of a flood, the pebbles settle once more and protect the sand and mud again. This is why rivers suddenly become muddy during a flood, and why the water quickly becomes clear afterwards.

The river's load

A river can carry many sorts of material. This is called the river's load (picture ②). During a flood the load contains pebbles that are being rolled along, sand that is hopping along near the bed, and silt and mud that has been made so fine it stays suspended in the water, giving it a muddy brown colour (picture ③). Some **DISSOLVED** material will be in the water, but normally it is invisible.

▼ ① When rivers flow fast, the bed forms ridges, called ripples, just like the ones you find on a beach. Sand hops along near the bottom of the bed from ripple to ripple. Mud can be swept along more easily because it is held up – suspended – in the water.

To understand how a pebble can become dissolved, try putting an antacid tablet in a glass of water and then add a few drops of vinegar. The tablet will begin to dissolve, and soon all that is left of what was once a solid tablet is a cloudy suspension of fine particles. The rest has dissolved and is invisible.

Pebbles take millions of times longer to dissolve than an antacid tablet, but, over time, almost everything can be dissolved by the natural acids in water. Mud is produced by the chemical dissolving action of water on rock.

▼ ② **These diagrams show that many kinds of material move in a river, often at the same time. Together, all the types of material are known as sediment.**

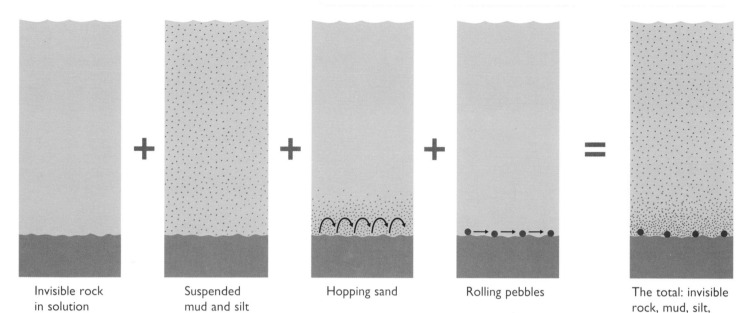

| Invisible rock in solution | Suspended mud and silt | Hopping sand | Rolling pebbles | The total: invisible rock, mud, silt, sand and pebbles |

► ③ **This river is carrying so much silt and mud that the water looks thick and brown. The brown colour is hiding the movement of the sand and pebbles. However, the person standing in the water could feel the pebbles knocking against his feet as they were rolled along.**

Waterfalls

A waterfall forms where a river plunges down a cliff.

A **WATERFALL** is the most dramatic feature in the course of a river. It is also unusual. Most rivers do not contain waterfalls. This is because waterfalls only form where the river flows over <u>flat</u> bands of hard and soft rock.

How a waterfall erodes

Rivers cannot easily cut through hard rock, but once they do, the softer rock below is rapidly removed.

You can see the way a waterfall works in picture ①. As the river water (and the pebbles it is carrying) falls down the face of a waterfall, it falls faster and faster. When it reaches the foot of the fall, it has great energy (picture ②).

The rock at the foot of the waterfall is worn away by pebbles in the falling and swirling water. This produces a deep pool, called a **PLUNGE POOL** (picture ③).

As the plunge pool grows, it cuts back into the waterfall cliff (picture ③), and in time forms an overhanging ledge, or **WATERFALL LIP**. Eventually, the lip is left overhanging so much that it collapses under its own weight. The waterfall lip then

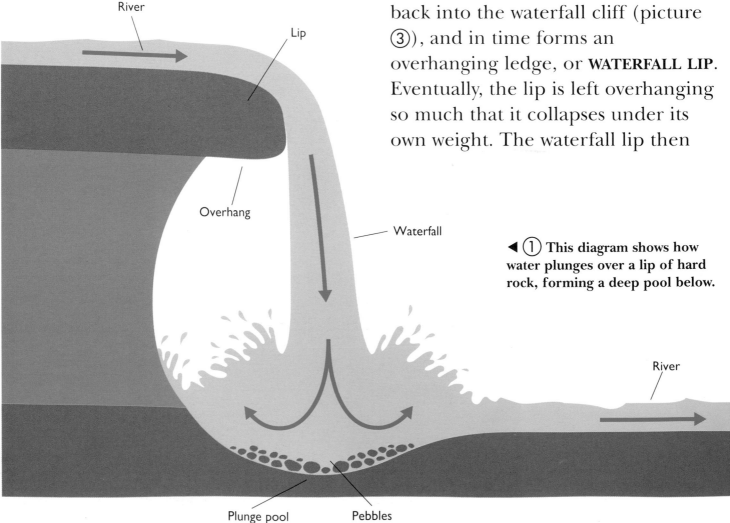

River

Lip

Overhang

Waterfall

◀ ① This diagram shows how water plunges over a lip of hard rock, forming a deep pool below.

River

Plunge pool

Pebbles

moves slightly back, and the process is repeated.

Often you can see a narrow gorge downstream of the waterfall (picture ③). This marks the place where the waterfall used to be. In time, as the waterfall continues to erode the rock, it will form a longer and longer gorge.

Rapids

It is quite rare for rocks to lie in flat (horizontal) bands. More often the rocks lie at a shallow angle and then **RAPIDS**, rather than waterfalls are produced. Rapids are also known as cataracts.

▲ ② This is a view of the lip of a waterfall. You can see that the water is flowing quite gently above the lip. The water then falls to the gorge below. You can imagine that any pebbles falling with the water will crack against the rocky bed below and cause more erosion.

▶ ③ This picture lets you see the difference in erosion of a river and a waterfall. Look closely at the river just above the fall and you will see a small gorge. This is what the river is able to do simply by flowing along a sloping course. But when the energy is concentrated, as in a waterfall, it can erode down much faster, as the gorge shows.

River meanders

Most rivers make loops, or meanders, over much of their courses.

Rivers flow in **CHANNELS**. Most rivers cut a single deep channel in a muddy bed. This channel winds its way across the flat floor of a valley. A large curve in a river is called a **MEANDER** (picture ①).

How meanders change

As water flows around a curve it gets thrown to the outside of the curve, rather like people on a spinning fairground ride feel themselves thrown outwards as the spin increases.

The river can scour its channel most quickly where it flows fastest, that is, near the outside of a bend. On the inside of the bend the water flows much more slowly.

The difference shows clearly in the depth of the water. It is deep on the outside of a bend and shallow on the inside (picture ②).

As the river cuts into the outside of the bend, and sand and mud settle out on the inside of the bend (picture ③). Thus, a river changes its shape but keeps the same width (picture ④).

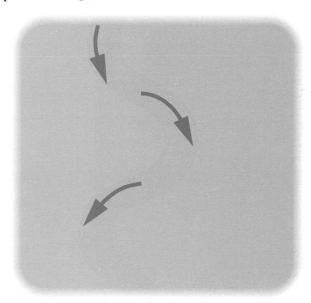

▲ ① This diagram shows a plan of a meander. The arrows show how water sweeps to the outside of each bend.

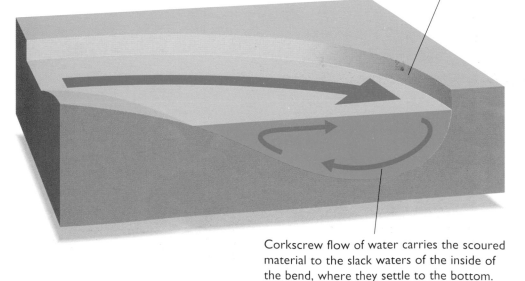

Scouring of the outside of bend produces a steep slope called a river cliff

Corkscrew flow of water carries the scoured material to the slack waters of the inside of the bend, where they settle to the bottom.

◀ ② The way that water in a meander flows around the outside of the bend, eroding the bend and making a steep side, or river cliff. The inside of the bend is shallow and gently sloping. It is called a slip-off slope. A balance between erosion on the outside and settling of mud, sand and pebbles on the inside keeps the river a constant width.

► ③ If you were to dip a jar into the water of a meandering river, this is what you would be likely to collect. The brown colour is caused by suspended mud. (See also the diagram and pictures on pages 14 and 15.)

▼ ④ This picture, taken from the air, shows a meandering stretch of a river. The river cliffs are on the outside of each bend. Notice how the insides of the bends have plants growing on them. This is where the sand and mud has recently been laid down, providing a fertile soil in which plants can begin to grow.

Oxbows

Oxbows are narrow-necked loops of a river. Oxbow lakes are oxbows that have been abandoned by a river, but still contain water.

A meander may grow into a very narrow-necked loop called an oxbow. Oxbows usually do not survive long. This is why.

As a river goes around the tight bend of an oxbow, the oxbow acts as a natural brake on the water (picture ①). This makes little difference for normal flows, but after a storm, when the river is running high, the tightness of an oxbow bend tends to make the water pile up rather than flow freely.

At these times the river may spill over the neck (the narrowest piece) of the oxbow and cut a new path, abandoning the oxbow completely.

An oxbow that has been abandoned is no longer scoured by the river. As a result, its ends quickly silt up and completely separate the oxbow loop from the river. However,

▼ ① **This diagram shows how a meander bend may become more and more pronounced until, during a flood, the oxbow is cut through and abandoned.**

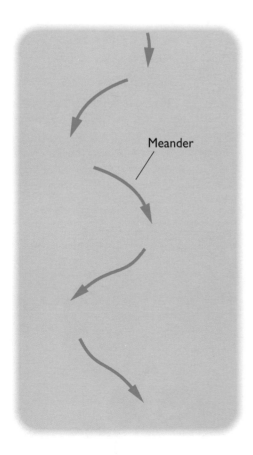

Meander

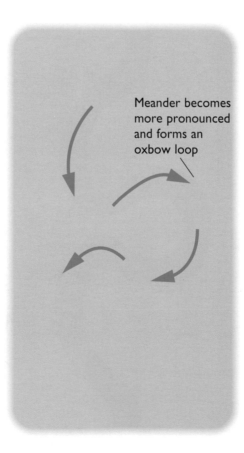

Meander becomes more pronounced and forms an oxbow loop

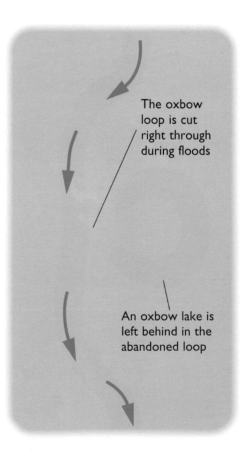

The oxbow loop is cut right through during floods

An oxbow lake is left behind in the abandoned loop

because it is at the same level as the river, water still tends to seep into the abandoned oxbow, creating a small **OXBOW LAKE**.

The best way of spotting oxbows and oxbow lakes is from the air (pictures ②, ③ and ④), but many also show up on maps.

▼ ② These oxbows and oxbow lakes have been highlighted to make them easier to see.

▼ ③ This picture shows an oxbow bend. Notice that it is an oxbow because the bend has a narrow neck.

▲ ④ There are several meanders on this meandering river. The nearest two are oxbows.

Shifting islands

Rivers that flow over a bed of gravel and pebbles have many shifting islands.

Most rivers contain only a few islands. Usually they are made of mud and fixed in place by the roots of trees. However, in some rivers, there are thousands of tiny shifting islands, made up of a loose mixture of sand, gravel and pebbles. Trees can rarely get a foothold in this material because there is no mud to stick the pebbles and gravel together. As a result, the islands often change shape.

Braided channels

Channels made of only sand, gravel and pebbles cannot make upright banks and so they are not deep. As a result, these rivers wash over broad regions of a valley, cutting many shallow, intertwining channels.

From above, the intertwining islands look a little like the strands of braided hair (pictures ① and ②).

This is why they are called **BRAIDED RIVERS**. Most braided rivers will be found in mountainous regions, because this is where pebbles and gravel are most common (pictures ③, ④ and ⑤).

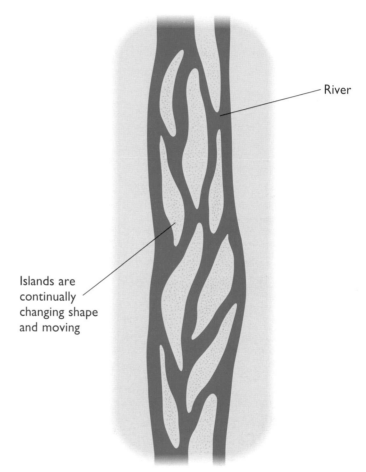

River

Islands are continually changing shape and moving

▲ ① The pattern of channels in a braided river.

▼ ② **A braided river often has many channels. Here you can see the channels in plan and as a side view. Notice that the channels are wide and shallow.**

The river is split into a number of shallow channels

The river bed is made of sand, gravel or pebbles

▲▼ Pictures ③ and ④ show braided rivers when the water level is low. It is easy to see the dividing islands. The rivers clearly have a wide channel that moves in an almost straight line through the valley bottom. As a result there is no meandering. Compare this to the pictures on page 21. Also, make sure you appreciate the size of these rivers. The trees by the river bank in the bottom picture, for example, are 50 m tall!

▲ ⑤ This picture shows the kind of gravel and pebble mixture that forms the dividing islands.

Lakes

Lakes are not formed by rivers, although they are commonly found in river valleys. Rivers are steadily filling in lakes throughout the world.

A **LAKE** is a large volume of still water that fills a natural basin in the landscape. Lake basins are the only part of a river's course that were not formed by the river. Instead, they were created by some other natural process which has since been filled by river water to make a lake (picture ①).

Ribbon lakes

Most long, narrow lakes fill deep trenches in the landscape. These trenches were scoured out by ancient glaciers. Many of these lakes are in mountain valleys, where the glaciers used to be (picture ②).

Because mountain lakes are narrow and fill the bottoms of long straight valleys, they are commonly called **RIBBON LAKES**. High up in mountains, small bowl-shaped lakes can also be found. These, too fill hollows scoured out by former glaciers. They are called corrie lakes, after a Scottish word for cauldron.

Large lakes

Large shallow lakes are usually formed behind natural earth dams. The Great Lakes of North America were formed, in part, by a natural

▼ ① **This diagram shows the three important parts of a lake. The water enters then slows down, forming a delta. The stillness of the lake then allows even mud to settle. Finally, clear water flows out of the far end. Because lakes filter sand and mud in this way, they eventually fill up and disappear.**

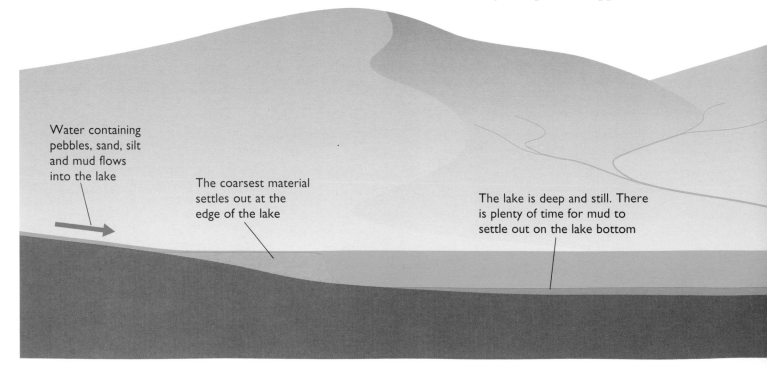

Water containing pebbles, sand, silt and mud flows into the lake

The coarsest material settles out at the edge of the lake

The lake is deep and still. There is plenty of time for mud to settle out on the lake bottom

earth dam of debris left behind at the end of the last Ice Age.

Large lakes are also sometimes produced when parts of the Earth's surface sinks. The lakes of East Africa fill parts of deep valleys called **RIFT VALLEYS**.

▼▶ ② This is a picture of Derwent Water in the English Lake District. Compare the picture with the diagram below to see how the lake works. The map on the right shows the location of Derwent Water.

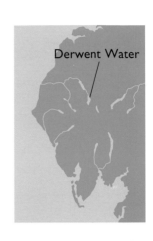
Derwent Water

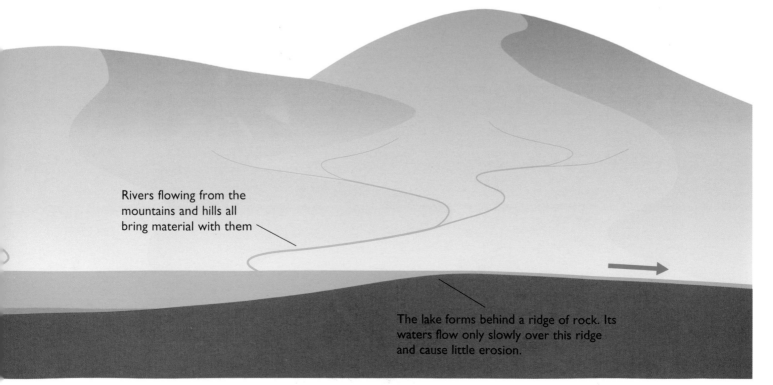

Rivers flowing from the mountains and hills all bring material with them

The lake forms behind a ridge of rock. Its waters flow only slowly over this ridge and cause little erosion.

Deltas and estuaries

Deltas are areas of flat land that form at the river's mouth or in a lake. An estuary is a river mouth that does not contain a delta.

When rivers reach the still waters of a sea or a lake, the river current slackens and much of the material being carried settles out.

The heavier sand or gravel settles out at the edge of the still water until finally it reaches the surface and new land is formed. This material is called a delta (picture ①).

The river flows over this newly built land, so that sand and gravel travels farther into the lake or sea before settling out. By continually carrying material to the edge of its delta, the river gradually builds the delta outwards.

Shapes of deltas

The most common shape of delta looks like an opened fan (picture ②). It has a regular edge. This shape forms when the river divides into a number of more or less equal channels, called **DISTRIBUTARIES**, as it flows over the delta. Each channel distributes a more of less equal amount of sand and gravel across the delta.

However, in some cases the main channel does not break up into distributaries. As a result, one part builds far faster than anywhere else. The shape of this type of delta is quite irregular (pictures ③ and ④).

Estuaries

An estuary is a river mouth that has been flooded by the sea. It will only be a matter of time before enough sand and mud is brought to the estuary by the river to produce a delta.

▼ ① This side view of a delta shows its nearly flat top and straight sloping front.

The river spreads out over its delta

As the water enters the lake or the sea, the sand spills over the delta and adds to the front of it.

The edge of the delta can be scoured by waves and water currents

▶ ② Fan-shaped delta. This kind of delta forms wherever channels spread out evenly across the delta. The example shown in the photograph is the Nile delta, northeast Africa.

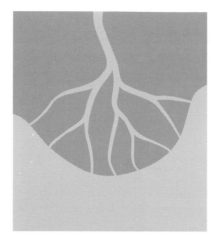 

▶ ③ Bird's-foot delta. This kind of delta forms when a single main channel changes direction frequently. This example is the Mississippi delta in the south of the United States. The light blue colour is actually sand and mud leaving the end of the delta and being washed about by ocean currents.

 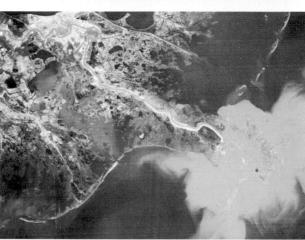

▼ ④ The bird's-foot delta of Derwent Water, Lake District. See how the delta is being colonised by plants. With their help, the older parts of the delta quickly come to look just the same as the nearby land.

Gorges

Gorges are deep valleys caused when rivers cut into the land very quickly.

Rivers flow in **VALLEYS**. A gorge is a special kind of valley – with vertical sides. The vertical sides mean that it is formed almost entirely by a river cutting into its bed.

Most valleys are not gorges – they have more gently sloping sides. Even a **CANYON** does not have sheer sides. This means there must be other processes at work in forming most valleys. You will see these on page 30.

How a gorge forms

A gorge is a valley with vertical sides cut into the land (picture ①). Gorges form wherever the river is itself the main cause of erosion. You find them especially in mountainous areas, near waterfalls and where rivers flow through deserts.

In each case the river flows quickly down a steep course and has lots of energy to cut into its bed. By contrast, the valley sides hardly change at all, perhaps because the rock is very hard, or perhaps because there is little rain. As a result the valley doesn't get wider, just deeper (picture ②).

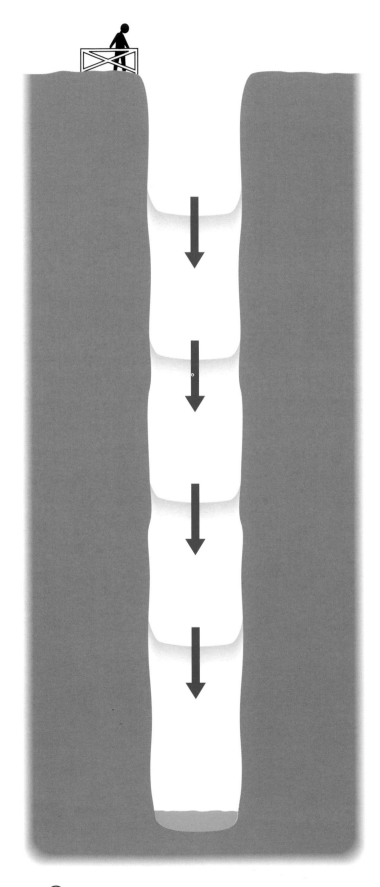

▲ ① This is the shape of a gorge. It is only being cut where the river flows.

▲ ② This picture shows the main features of a gorge. Notice that the water flows across the entire width of the gorge floor, wearing it away evenly. The gorge also has sheer sides that have no plants growing on them. A few large blocks of rock have fallen away from the gorge walls and lie in the bottom. They will be worn away during times of high water.

Upper valleys

In the upper part of its course, a river flows in a steep-sided, twisting valley.

If you were to make a journey from the source to the mouth of a river, you would find that the valley had a different shape near its source, from the shape in the middle of its course, to the shape near the sea. People often talk of these parts of a valley as upper valley, middle valley and lower valley.

In the upper part of its course, a river is usually flowing swiftly, following a steeply sloping path. The sides of the valley are steep and straight, and landslides, mudflows and even rockfalls are common.

Look up or down such a valley and you can see that the shape is like a letter V, so these valleys are often called **V-SHAPED VALLEYS** (pictures ① and ②).

The river twists about but there is no flat floor, so it doesn't form meanders – these will form in the middle course.

The winding path cuts in and out of the land, so that when you look up or down a valley, the river is sometimes hidden from view by valley slopes jutting out. The slopes are

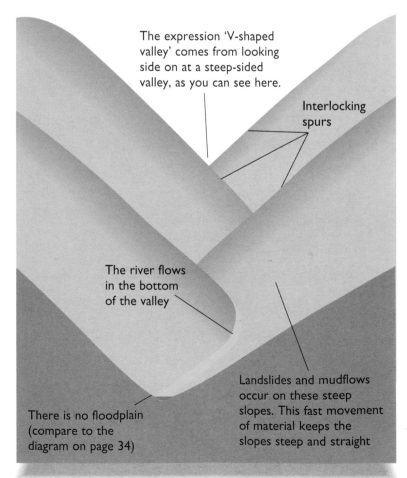

The expression 'V-shaped valley' comes from looking side on at a steep-sided valley, as you can see here.

Interlocking spurs

The river flows in the bottom of the valley

Landslides and mudflows occur on these steep slopes. This fast movement of material keeps the slopes steep and straight

There is no floodplain (compare to the diagram on page 34)

◄ ① **The main features of the upper course of a valley are shown on this picture.**

▲ ② **This valley shows how many kinds of movement can go on at the same time. On the left hand slope there is no soil. During the winter the rock is attacked by frost and shattered into pieces that later slide down the valley side and into the river.**

The opposite slope is forested. Frost cannot get to the rock on this slope, so soil will form and landslides and mudflows will be common.

called spurs. When you look down a valley, the spurs come alternately from left, then right, in other words they interlock. Thus they are called **INTERLOCKING SPURS** (picture ③).

▼ ③ The main upper valley features are shown on this picture. Look for the interlocking spurs and the V-shape made by the sides.

This picture shows the river during summer when the water level is low. In winter the water fills the entire channel.

Pebbles in the bed show that the river sometimes has enough energy to move large material.

Middle valleys

By the time the river reaches the middle valley, it is flowing down a less steep path than in its upper course.

The most obvious features of the middle valley are the flat valley floor, or **FLOODPLAIN**, and the way that the river meanders (picture ①).

Compare these pictures with those on the previous page and you will see the important differences. For example, if you look down a valley in its middle course, you will notice that the spurs no longer reach across and interlock. Instead there is a wide flat strip (the floodplain) on either side of the river.

The floodplain

The floodplain (pictures ② and ③) is a flat area of land on either side of the river that contains mud, silt, sand and pebbles brought down from the upper valley. As the meanders change position across the valley bottom, they produce the flat surface of the floodplain. This flat, low-lying land is easily flooded, which is why it is called a floodplain.

The valley shape

It is less easy to see the middle valley as a V-shaped valley. The slopes are less steep and the centre of the valley contains the flat floodplain.

Landslides and mudflows are uncommon in the middle course of the valley. For the most part, soils simply creep downslope or are dissolved by water in the soil and carried away in solution.

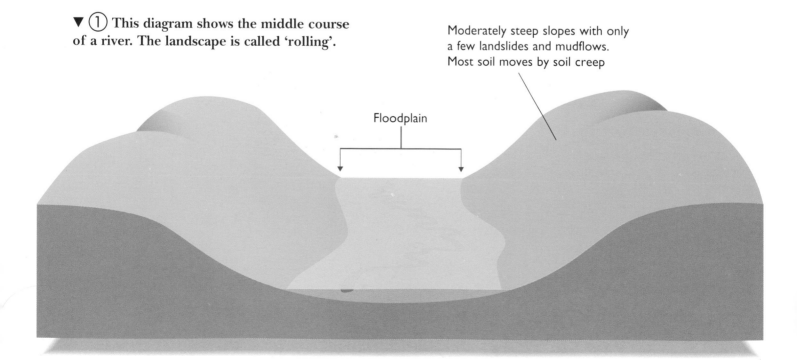

▼ ① This diagram shows the middle course of a river. The landscape is called 'rolling'.

Moderately steep slopes with only a few landslides and mudflows. Most soil moves by soil creep

Floodplain

▼ ② The floodplain is where pebbles, sand and mud are stored between floods. During this time it remains wet and slowly rots into mud.

During a flood, the river carries some of its store of material downstream. At the same time new material arrives from the upper valley. In this way the material in the floodplain is regularly changed.

►▼ ③ In some valleys the floodplain appears to have steps in it. You can see a step in the picture on the right. Steps in the bottom of a valley are called RIVER TERRACES. Each terrace was once a floodplain of the river before the river cut down quickly and began cutting a new floodplain. River terraces are good places to build houses because they are flat, close to the river, and yet safe from flooding.

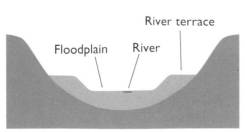

River terrace

Floodplain   River

Lower valleys

The lower course of a river has a wide floodplain that merges into very gentle valley sides. Wide meanders with oxbows and levees can form here.

In the lower course of a river the valley is very wide and shallow and the landscape has no steep slopes (picture ①).

The river is so close to the level of the sea that it hardly cuts into its bed at all. Instead, it meanders widely from side to side cutting a broad floodplain and sometimes leaving oxbow lakes.

Levees

During floods, water spills out over the floodplain and flows much more slowly. Any sand and silt carried on to the floodplain will settle close to the river. This is because sand and silt are quite heavy.

Sand and silt may build up to make a wide low natural earth bank or **LEVEE** (picture ②). Rivers that carry large amounts of sand and silt are common in, for example, Australia, the United States, China and South Africa. The Mississippi in the United States (picture ③) and the Huang He (Yellow River) in China contain the world's biggest levees.

If the river carries mostly mud (as is the case in most of the United Kingdom, Ireland, Canada, New Zealand etc.), levees will not form and the mud will be deposited evenly over the floodplain.

Estuaries and deltas

A river ends its lower course at the sea. Here it may enter an estuary or form a delta at the coast.

▼ ① This diagram shows the lower course of a river. The landscape is almost flat.

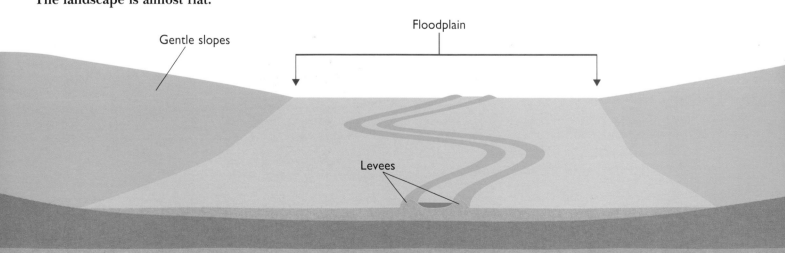

Gentle slopes

Floodplain

Levees

When there is no delta, this tells us that, in the recent past, the sea level has risen quickly, drowning the coastal part of the river valley. Since then, there has not been enough time for the drowned part of the valley to fill completely with mud and sand. There are many reasons for this, but many coastal parts of valleys were drowned at the end of the last Ice Age, which was only about 10,000 years ago.

▶ ② The Mississippi river near New Orleans, USA. This is one of the world's mightiest rivers, with great sweeping meanders in its lower valley.

The floodplain is too wide to show in this photograph, so everything you see is floodplain. The long grassy ridges close to the river are levees. They are partly natural, but they have been made artificially higher to help prevent flooding.

▲ ③ This is the Missouri river north of St Louis, USA. The wide flat floodplain is in the background. The brown colour of the water shows that the river is carrying much material as fine silt and mud.

Floods

Floods occur when rivers spill over their banks after prolonged or heavy rain. Often the whole floodplain turns into a shallow lake.

River channels are not often overtopped. But after a long period of rain, a heavy downpour, or when snow melts rapidly, the water reaching the river is so great that the channel fills up completely and soon after the river bursts its banks. This is a flood.

In many parts of the world flooding occurs, on average, about once every three years.

Flooding has a different effect in each part of the valley. In the narrow upper course, flooding can occur very suddenly because water is more likely to flow quickly off the steep slopes. There is little flat land by the river to store the floodwater and, as a result, the floodwater quickly moves down the valley. This sometimes happens so quickly it is called a **FLASH FLOOD**.

In the middle course the valley has a wide floodplain (picture ①). Water spreads over the floodplain, creating what is really a large, shallow lake. The lake is slow to fill and slow to drain and as a result, floods may rise slowly but they may last for many days.

In the lower course, where the floodplain is widest of all, floods take longest of all to creep up over the floodplain (pictures ②, and ③). They are also the slowest to subside. It may take weeks for such floods to drain away.

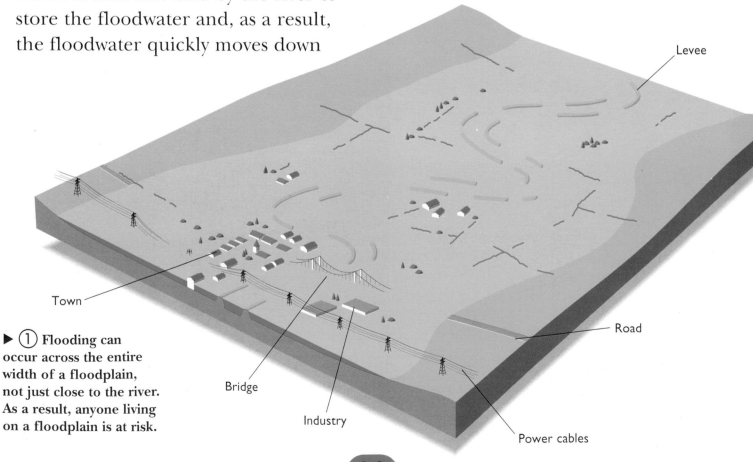

► ① **Flooding can occur across the entire width of a floodplain, not just close to the river. As a result, anyone living on a floodplain is at risk.**

Levee

Town

Bridge

Industry

Road

Power cables

38

◀ ② You don't have to be within sight of a river to suffer a flood. It is quite common for floodwaters to rise 10 to 15 metres above normal during a flood, allowing floodwaters to reach very large areas. This picture shows a house half submerged in a floodplain 'lake'.

▼ ③ This is a picture of the Mississippi in flood in its middle course. The floodplain is very wide and flooding spreads out over a very large area. Only the bridges mark where the river normally flows.

Coping with floods

Floods cause great damage and thus much effort goes into flood protection.

Floods need not worry us at all if we choose to live away from the river. But the land near the river is easiest for building and best for farming. As a result, people have always had to live with the risk of floods destroying their crops or their homes (picture ①).

Flood and mud

When many people think of floods, they think only of water. Anyone who has ever had to cope with a flood disaster knows different (picture ②). A flood consists of <u>two</u> parts: <u>water</u> and <u>the material it is carrying</u>. This is often mud which sticks to everything inside a flooded house and makes clearing up miserable.

How to protect homes

Many towns and cities and even farmland are protected by man-made levees (picture ③). They need to be higher than the expected height of floodwaters and strong enough to stand up to the pressure from floodwaters.

There are some other ways of stopping flooding. One way is to build a **DAM** and **RESERVOIR** along the courses of flood-prone rivers. Deep, narrow valleys are the easiest places to build dams. River water can be stored in the reservoir until the threat of flooding is past. The water can then be slowly released from the reservoir.

Where dams are not possible, the best solution is to make sure as much water seeps into soil and as little as possible goes into drains, for then there will be less water rushing quickly into the rivers.

▲ ① Floods often occur in upper parts of valleys where there are no floodplains. Rivers flood quickly and carry boulders big enough to smash houses. There is little that can be done for protection.

▲ ② This picture shows the clearing-up operation after a flood. The main battle is to remove the clinging mud.

▶ ③ These people are filling sandbags which will be carried to a nearby levee to help prevent it from collapsing. Look into the distance and see the thousands of people involved and you begin to get a sense of the massive task in trying to prevent flooding.

Water supply

Everyone must have water to drink. People also need water for many other uses, such as washing and cooking. Most of this has to be supplied by rivers.

How much water is there in our rivers? In times of flood there seems far too much. But when there is a drought, it becomes obvious that there can also be too little for our needs. So how do we use our rivers, and how can we make better use of them?

Using water more than once

Think of the uses for water (picture ①). Of course drinking water is vital, but it is a tiny amount compared with the water used to wash up, to flush the toilet, wash out clothes and so on.

Water is used in factories and offices as well. And it is used to cool

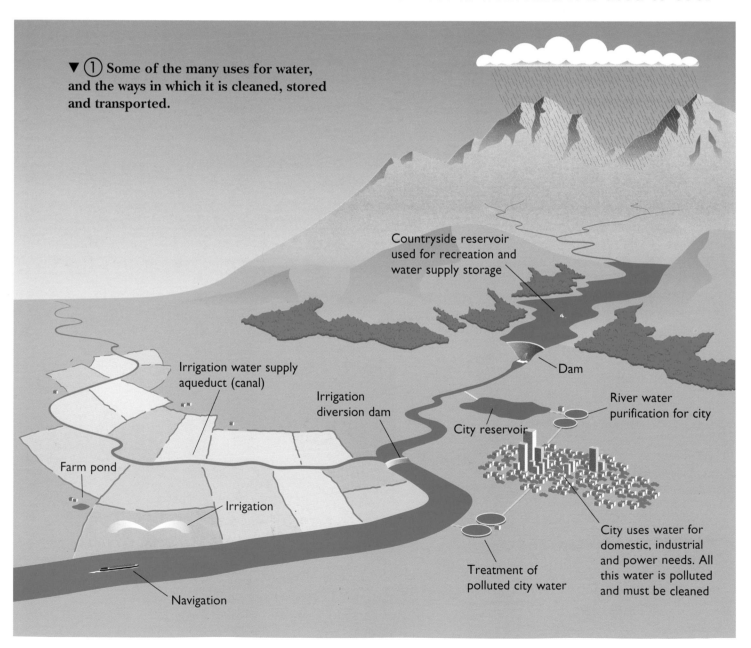

▼ ① Some of the many uses for water, and the ways in which it is cleaned, stored and transported.

Countryside reservoir used for recreation and water supply storage

Dam

River water purification for city

Irrigation water supply aqueduct (canal)

Irrigation diversion dam

City reservoir

Farm pond

Irrigation

City uses water for domestic, industrial and power needs. All this water is polluted and must be cleaned

Treatment of polluted city water

Navigation

power stations, for transportation and to provide us with recreation (pictures ② and ③).

Another very important use of water is for **IRRIGATING** during a dry spell (picture ④).

With all of these uses we do, in fact, use more water than the rivers contain! The only reason rivers keep flowing is because we put most of it back.

▲ ② **A dam being used to hold back water in a reservoir to prevent flooding and so that it can be used to supply water in times of little rainfall.**

◀ ③ **People fishing in a river for recreation.**

Making river water clean

Does it horrify you to know that the water you drink has been used by several other people? It shouldn't because all water has been used countless times. This is why the way water moves is called a water cycle.

The reason we can use water again and again is because it is naturally purified whenever it evaporates from oceans or when it seeps through the ground. Rivers and lakes also purify water. So each part of the water cycle has a way of making dirty water clean.

It would not, however, be safe to drink water from most rivers today. This is because nature's purifying arrangements cannot cope with the amount of waste that people now produce. This is why we use purification works for all water pumped out of rivers, and why we clean the water again before it is returned to the river after use.

▲ ④ **Irrigation is one of the main uses for water in many drier countries. Here irrigation water is being distributed onto a field using a spray system that is rolled across the fields.**

The world's biggest rivers

AFRICA

The world's longest river is the Nile in East Africa, stretching 6670 km from the Equator to the Mediterranean sea. Many people think of the Nile as an 'Egyptian' river, but it begins far to the south, near the Equator.

The Nile has two main sources: one starts in Lake Victoria and is known as the White Nile; the other starts in the Ethiopian Highlands and is called the Blue Nile. The White and Blue Nile join at the Sudanese capital of Khartoum. From here the Nile flows through desert and no more water enters.

During its next 1800 km the river sweeps in a great S-shaped path. On it lie some rapids (or cataracts). The most famous is at the city of Aswan now the site of the Aswan High Dam which ponds a gigantic reservoir called Lake Nasser which has flooded part of the Nile valley.

SOUTH AMERICA

The Amazon is the world's biggest river by volume of water discharged even though, at 6450 km, it is not quite as long as Africa's Nile. This is because the Amazon is fed by a network of smaller, or tributary, rivers that cover more than half of South America – over one-twentieth of the world's entire land area!

The drainage basin of the Amazon covers seven billion square kilometres, with 15,000 major tributary rivers. Its largest tributary, the Rio Madeira, is the world's fourteenth longest river.

When it reaches the Atlantic Ocean, the Amazon is carrying more than one-fifth of all the water that flows in the world's rivers.

◄ Niagara Falls, Canada.

There are many sources to the Amazon. Most lie in the west of the continent, on the flanks of the giant Andes mountain range in areas that are tropical forest. In these places rain falls throughout the year and it soaks readily into the soils to feed the river. The Andes is the only place where waterfalls occur in the Amazon basin.

Except in the Andes, the Amazon flows in a giant low lying basin, the vast majority of it being less than 150 metres above sea level. This means that the valley sides are rarely seen, and the river simply winds aimlessly over a huge floodplain. Near the sea the river is over 160 km wide and its mouth is studded with low muddy islands. When you stand on one bank it is impossible to see the other side.

The tides, and salty water, reach upstream for 1000 km, which is farther than any other river in the world.

NORTH AMERICA

The Mississippi (3800 km) is the longest river in North America but it is only the tenth longest river in the world. It is, however, one of the world's muddiest rivers. The Mississippi delta, where much of the mud comes to rest, juts out into the Gulf of Mexico downstream of the city of New Orleans.

ASIA

The River Ganges makes the biggest delta (75,000 square kilometres) as it enters the Bay of Bengal in Bangladesh and northeast India.

The world's muddiest river is the Huang He (4850 km) in China. It carries so much silt that the river is always a yellow-brown colour. For this reason it is also called the Yellow River. The Huang He has dropped so much silt on its bed that it now flows many metres above the surrounding land, often flooding and causing great loss of life. For this reason the river is also known as 'China's sorrow'.

AUSTRALASIA

The longest river in Australia is the Murray (2589 km).

EUROPE

Europe's longest river is the Volga which runs south through Russia to the Caspian Sea for 3690 km.

Glossary

ABRASION The wearing away of a river bed by the scouring action of pebbles.

AQUEDUCT An artificial channel designed to carry water for use in homes, industry and farms.

ATTRITION The wearing away of pebbles as they bump into each other while moving in a river.

BRAIDED RIVERS River channels with many low islands made of gravel and pebbles.

CANYON A very steep-sided river valley, usually found in desert areas.

CHANNEL The trench in which a river flows. If a channel's bed and banks are made of mud, it will be deep; if they are made of pebbles the channel will be shallow and contain many islands.

CLIFF A vertical slope, usually with a rocky face.

DAM A man-made barrier across a river designed to make an artificial lake.

DELTA The fan-shaped area of land that builds up where a river enters a sea or lake.

DISSOLVED MATERIAL Rock that has been dissolved and put into solution.

DISTRIBUTARIES Small channels that flow over a delta.

DROUGHT A long period without rain.

DYKE An earth wall. Another word for levee.

EDDY A whirling movement of water.

EROSION The wearing away and removal of land.

ESTUARY The coastal part of a drowned river valley containing sea water.

EVAPORATION When liquid water turns into vapour.

FLASH FLOOD A flood that happens within a few minutes after a heavy downpour of rain.

FLOOD When a river bursts its banks.

FLOODPLAIN The flat land to either side of a river that is made of materials deposited by the river during floods.

GORGE A narrow river valley with vertical sides.

GULLIES Small trenches in the soil formed by running water.

HEADWATERS The place where the river has its source.

INTERLOCKING SPURS Parts of the valley sides that jut out part way across the valley, alternately from the left and right-hand sides.

IRRIGATION Watering farmland.

LAKE A natural hollow in which river water is stored.

LEVEE A natural or man-made earth bank next to, and parallel to the river channel.

LOWER VALLEY A valley with a wide floodplain in a landscape of gentle slopes.

MEANDER A big curve in a river's course which only forms on floodplains.

MIDDLE VALLEY A valley with a floodplain in a landscape with moderately steep hillslopes

MUD Tiny minerals made by the chemical rotting of rock in water are called clay. The clay readily sticks together to form mud.

OXBOW LAKES Abandoned loops of river meanders.

PEBBLE A smooth stone that has been worn by movement in a river.

PLUNGE POOL The hollow scoured out by pebbles at the bottom of a waterfall.

POTHOLE A hole drilled in the bed of a river by swirling pebbles. (Do not confuse a river pothole with a caver's word for a hole where water sinks into the ground which is also called a pothole, or more correctly, a swallow hole.)

RAPIDS A swift flow of water over bands of hard rock that jut up from the river bed.

RECLAIM LAND To turn land that was once river bed into land for living on.

RESERVOIR An artificial lake held behind a dam.

RIBBON LAKE A long, narrow lake in a mountain valley.

RIFT VALLEYS Valleys caused by a downward movement of part of the Earth's surface.

RIVER BASIN The area drained by a river and its tributaries.

RIVER TERRACES Natural 'benches' just above a modern floodplain that show the level of ancient floodplains. River terraces are often used as dry sites for towns and cities.

SAND Fragments of rock about the same size as sugar grains.

SCAR A bare patch of ground showing where soil used to be.

SILT Fragments of rock about the same size as dust.

SOIL CREEP The slow movement of soil down a steep slope.

SOURCE The place where the river starts, perhaps in a spring.

SPRING A place where water seeps out of soil or rock to make a stream.

TRIBUTARIES Small parts, or branches, of a stream or river that join others to make a larger river.

UPPER VALLEY A valley with steep v-shaped sides and no floodplain

VALLEY A long trench in the landscape. In a river valley, the sides slope down to the river channel.

V-SHAPED VALLEY A river valley with straight sides that looks like a letter V.

WATER CYCLE The constant flow of water from rivers to the sea to the air and back to the land again.

WATER PURIFICATION Making river water fit to drink.

WATER SUPPLY The business of providing us with the water we need.

WATERFALL A fall of water over a ledge of hard rock.

WATERFALL LIP The ledge of hard rock at a waterfall.

Index